# LET'S GET MARRIED!

## WEDDING PLANNING GUIDE & ORGANIZER

# TIMELINE

## First Priorities
**12** Guest list, budget, venue and overall theme

## Essential Vendors
**11** Photographer, videographer, musicians

## Lay the Groundwork
**10** Website, stationery, plan for out-of-town guests

## Save the Date!
**9** Save the Dates, wedding dress, event schedule

## Florals and Wedding Party
**8** Wedding party, select your florist

## Welcoming Your Guests
**7** Rehearsal dinner, welcome party, rentals

## A Little Breather
**6** Honeymoon planning, budget check in, gift registry

## Suits & Transportation
**5** Plan transportation logistics and buy the suit

## Tasty Tasks
**4** Final tasting, wedding cake, wedding rings

## Begin Finalizing
**3** Vows, finalize the menu, hire officiant, send invitations

## Party Essentials
**2** Dress fitting, marriage license, wedding party gifts

## Organize & Delegate
**1** Venue walk-through, seating chart, choose point person

## Get Married!
You did it! Congratulations, go let your hair down!

# Congratulations!

## HOW TO USE THIS GUIDE: TAKE IT ONE STEP AT A TIME

First of all, congratulations on your engagement! As you settle into the idea that you'll soon be married, it's probably sinking in just how intense this planning process is about to become. Overwhelmed by all the moving parts? Worried you'll forget something major? Nervous about how to feed all these people? It's going to be alright!

Use this concise yet detailed guide to make sure the essentials are covered with time to spare. The small stuff won't slip through the cracks and you'll be able to maintain your sanity and enjoy the process. It is my hope that you find joy in each step along the way.

Keep in mind this is just a guide. Weddings are changing along with the times. Today more than ever, couples are finding creative ways to share an unforgettable moment that celebrates their own, unique love story with their nearest and dearest in a very personal way.

Take it from a pro: there will be intense moments when you feel the pressure. Each section has tips to save you time, money and head space. If you're hitting a wall and things just aren't clicking - especially with a tight budget - step away for a breather. There's almost always an alternative means of getting your vision off the ground.

People love weddings! Your friends and family must be over the moon for you. Be sure to lean on them for help, but also be aware of the pitfalls of caving into others' expectations. You'll be pulled in many directions, but this day is ultimately about **you** and your other half.

This guide includes just a bit of room for you to jot down essential notes. My full-size wedding planning notebook *Let's Do This!* is the companion to this guide. It is a full planning journal with space for brainstorming, interview notes for all vendors, seating charts, guest lists, budgets and more. If you're a pen & paper person, consider *Let's Do This* as your workbook, journal and keepsake!

## MAKE THE TIMELINE WORK FOR YOU

Couples typically take anywhere from three to eighteen months to plan their wedding. This guide takes care of the highest priority and least flexible tasks first, using a 12-month timeline as its template. If you have more time, great! If you're on a time crunch, treat the timeline as a prioritized checklist. Tackle the top items first and work your way down.

I suggest flipping through this book to get familiar with each step of the process. The method laid out here is tried and true, but you are planning your own unique event and there will certainly be variations.

## GIVE YOURSELF ROOM TO BREATHE

There is no one-size-fits-all wedding guide, so I've left room for flexibility. See anything in here you won't be needing? Cross it out and forget it. Repurposing any tired traditions in exchange for your fresh take? There are tips and blank space throughout so you can pencil in *your* priorities.

## GO IT ALONE? OR HIRE A PLANNER?

Once your budget and overall theme is worked out, it wouldn't hurt to interview a few wedding planners. Depending on your preferences, they may not *save* you money, but their preferential rates with vendors could easily make up for their planning fee. Plus they'll be able to draw up the budget early on, and the organizational prowess of a professional can be invaluable.

Let's say you are dead set on going it alone. I'm with you! I've done it twice myself. Especially true if you're planning an inter-faith, cross cultural, or any alternative to the typical wedding, it could be difficult for a wedding planner to fully comprehend your vision. If you're a resourceful DIYer, you will find plenty of ways to avoid wedding prices while making your event all the more intimate and personal.

In summary, planning your wedding is no small task, but staying organized is half the battle. Now, go get planning. And make sure you and your better half enjoy the process!

# FIRST PRIORITIES
## Style, Guest List, Budget & Venue

### DRAW UP YOUR TIMELINE

The timeline at the front of this book is the ideal planning structure. However, you might have less or more time, or prioritize differently.

### GET CLEAR ON YOUR OVERALL THEME

Start by imagining the big day. What is the venue like? How is it decorated? What kind of food is being served? Who is in attendance and what is the vibe? Think about where you met, your favorite places, the people in your life. There's a sheet in this section with some common ideas to get your creative juices flowing. Circle, cross out, and get imaginative about the look and feel of your perfect wedding. Make a note of your must-haves and take it from there.

### CREATE THE GUEST LIST

Work together to jot down everyone you would consider inviting to the wedding. Putting this list together can be daunting and you're bound to forget people, so take a few passes. It could help to go through any chat history, emails, social media accounts - anything that jogs your memory.

### DRAFT YOUR BUDGET

Least glamorous yet most important of all tasks, the budget. As you get into the nitty gritty, remember that wedding guests tend to be generous gift givers, and consider any family contributions that could come into play. Beyond the large items like venue and catering, the smaller details will add up quickly. Get a realistic idea of how much you'll have to spend. The budget sheet in this section has all standard expenses itemized. You can probably omit some of these while others may benefit from more detail.

# MONTH 12

- Get clear on the overall style
- Create guest list
- Make the budget
- Choose a venue and caterer
- _____

### NOTES

| MONDAY | TUESDAY | WEDNESDAY | THURSDAY | FRIDAY | SATURDAY | SUNDAY |
|--------|---------|-----------|----------|--------|----------|--------|
|        |         |           |          |        |          |        |
|        |         |           |          |        |          |        |
|        |         |           |          |        |          |        |
|        |         |           |          |        |          |        |
|        |         |           |          |        |          |        |

### EVENTS

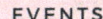

### PRO TIP

Once the word "wedding" is uttered, fees could surge. If you're shopping non-traditional spaces and vendors, try not to mention that it's your wedding until after you've negotiated rates.

# WEDDING STYLE
*Theme Worksheet*

## WHAT'S YOUR VIBE?

| | | | |
|---|---|---|---|
| Outdoor | Fresh | Eco-Friendly | Let Loose |
| Indoor | Sleek | Rustic | Understated |
| Urban | Non-Traditional | Cozy | Formal |
| Country | Family Focused | Industrial | Laid Back |
| Waterside | Friend Focused | Chic | Tropical |
| Great View | Religious | Bohemian | Casual |
| Garden | Traditional | Alternative | Intimate |
| Sophisticated | Multi-Cultural | Classic | Colorful |

## CATERING, FOOD AND DRINKS

| | | | |
|---|---|---|---|
| Buffet | Cocktail Hour | Locally-Sourced | Beer & Wine |
| Family Style | Food Truck | Grazing Boards | Cash Bar |
| Plated Dinner | Sig. Cocktails | Full Bar | Open Bar |
| Cocktail Party | Slushies | Champagne Toast | Self-Serve |
| BBQ Station | Shots | Flaming Dessert | Non-Alcoholic |

## MUSIC AND ENTERTAINMENT

| | | | |
|---|---|---|---|
| Ceremony | DJ | Photo Booth | First Dance |
| Reception | Live Band | Kids Activities | Games |
| Welcome Party | Singer | Fire Dancer | Glitter Bar |

# SAMPLE GUEST LIST

| NAME/FAMILY | GUEST COUNT | ATTENDING |
|---|---|---|
| | | Y / N |
| | | Y / N |
| | | Y / N |
| | | Y / N |
| | | Y / N |
| | | Y / N |
| | | Y / N |
| | | Y / N |
| | | Y / N |
| | | Y / N |
| | | Y / N |
| | | Y / N |
| | | Y / N |
| | | Y / N |
| | | Y / N |
| | | Y / N |
| | | Y / N |
| | | Y / N |
| | | Y / N |
| | | Y / N |
| | | Y / N |
| | | Y / N |
| **Total** | | Y / N |

# MASTER BUDGET

| DESCRIPTION | BUDGET | ACTUAL COST | DEPOSIT |
|---|---|---|---|
| **Venue Rental** | | | |
| Welcome / Rehearsal Dinner | | | |
| Ceremony | | | |
| Reception | | | |
| **Catering** | | | |
| Welcome / Rehearsal Dinner | | | |
| Reception | | | |
| Rentals | | | |
| Wedding Attire | | | |
| Music & Entertainment | | | |
| Flowers | | | |
| Non-floral Decorations | | | |
| Photographer / Videographer | | | |
| Officiant & Marriage License | | | |
| Stationery | | | |
| Wedding Rings | | | |
| Gifts for the Wedding Party | | | |
| Hair & Makeup | | | |
| Wedding Cake | | | |
| Party Favors | | | |
| Transportation | | | |
| Tips / Gratuities | | | |
| **Total** | | | |

# WEDDING PLANNER

## Key Questions to Ask

- How many weddings have you planned?
- Can you work within my budget?
- Any photos of previous work you have done in this style?
- What is your experience planning weddings like mine?
- What services do you offer? (full service, a la carte, day-of coordination)
- How many meetings will we have and how will I be involved?
- How can you see us achieving our vision at this venue?
- How involved will we be in the vendor selection process?
- Will you handle the contracts and vendor payments directly?
- How many of your staff will be at the wedding?
- By when do we need to finalize the details?
- What is the deposit and when is the final payment due?
- How does your payment structure work?
- Are there any anticipated expenses on top of what we have discussed?

## COST SHEET

| | |
|---|---|
| Planning fee | $ |
| A la carte rate | $ |
| Day-of Coordination | $ |
| Extras | $ |
| | $ |
| | $ |
| **Total** | $ |

# VENUE & CATERING

### SELECTING A VENUE

Don't shy away from thinking outside the box here. Couples are increasingly turning to non-traditional venues for a more personalized and intimate event. Villas on Airbnb and unused industrial spaces can be great as long as they allow events. When comparing venues, your main concern should be practicality: can your caterer, florist, decorator, and musicians work with the space? Be sure to ask about extra event fees.

### CHOOSING THE RIGHT CATERER

Gone are the days when a plated dinner is expected at a wedding. Couples are increasingly opting for a more laid-back approach, be it family style, buffet, or even a cocktail-style reception. Food trucks and flaming dessert carts aren't uncommon for late-night snacks. Food and drinks will make up a massive part of your budget and will stick in everyone's memory of the night, so whichever way you go about feeding your guests, make sure you're loving it.

### PRO TIP

Book your venue and caterer at the same time. They are intricately linked and this could be a great opportunity to save yourself time, stress and money down the road if you're certain they are compatible.

### BUDGET TIPS

If you're going with an alternative venue & caterer, think about plates, glasses, silverware, decorations, etc. These might be cheaper to buy and use once rather than rent. See if you can recycle or resell them after the wedding.

If you don't want to skimp on booze but your budget disagrees, book a venue that allows you to supply your own alcohol and source it from a wholesaler with a bottle deposit fee.

# VENUE MEETING

Venue:                                Contact Person:

---

- How many weddings do you do in a typical year?
- What is the maximum capacity?
- How many hours are included in the rental?
- How early can vendors arrive for deliveries and set up?
- Will staff help receive deliveries, set up and break down?
- Do you have in-house catering?
- Is food & beverage included in the rental fee? Any minimums?
- Can we supply our own alcohol?
- Are there any restrictions on using outside vendors?
- Do you have sound equipment and microphones?
- Is there guest parking onsite or a valet?
- What is the payment schedule and what is included in the total?
- Any additional charges like corkage, cake cutting, service, etc.
- When is the deposit and final payment due?

## COST SHEET

| | |
|---|---|
| Venue rental fee | $ |
| Staff | $ |
| Furniture & equipment rental | $ |
| Permits or any extra fees | $ |
| Food & Beverage estimate (if venue will provide catering) | $ |
| Any extras | $ |
| **Total** | $ |

# NOTES

# CATERER MEETING

Caterer: Contact Person:

---

- Do you have any other obligations on our date?
- Do you have sufficient staff to cover all events that day?
- How much time will you need for set up and break down?
- Will there be an onsite coordinator on the day-of?
- Have you catered a wedding at our venue before?
- Can you achieve our vision at this venue?
- Are you able to provide linens, table settings, etc.?
- If not, will you handle coordinating the rentals?
- Are there any delivery fees for the rentals?
- Can we supply our own alcohol?
- Are your bartenders able to make specialty cocktails?
- Any special event permits required? Will you handle this?
- When is the final menu decision needed by?
- When is the final payment due?

## COST SHEET

| | |
|---|---|
| Cocktail hour / passed hors d'oeuvres | $ |
| Dinner | $ |
| Beverages | $ |
| Staff | $ |
| Gratuity | $ |
| Any extras | $ |
| **Total** | $ |

# NOTES

# 11 MONTHS
## Hire the Essential Vendors

### GET MUSICAL

Music makes the magic happen. If you've got a particular band, DJ, or vibe in mind, it's best to make introductions early. Say you're creating your own playlist - why not add a few guests with trustworthy musical taste to join in on the creation? You'll likely be focused on the reception, so don't forget about the ceremony music!

### PHOTOGRAPHER & VIDEOGRAPHER

If it's done well, you will likely find yourself re-watching your wedding footage for years to come. Learn the photographer's and videographer's style and be very clear on the tone, style and theme you'd like for the photos and video. Your crew should ask proactively, but make sure they know your priorities: exchanging vows, the first dance, your closest friends and relatives, etc. It's best if you *click* with this crew because they'll be your own personal paparazzi all night.

### ENTERTAINMENT

Easily omitted if it doesn't fit into your vision of the big day, but as weddings adapt to today's trends, couples are exploring ways to *wow* their guests. Fire dancers, photo booths, and palm readers are a few ideas. If there are children in attendance, it could be nice to keep them occupied, especially during the ceremony.

 You might find a photographer in your area on social media that doesn't typically shoot weddings. You'll have to make sure they're able to handle the burden of wedding photography but may snag a deal and get unique shots for your wedding album by hiring an emerging talent!

# MONTH 11

## TO-DOS

Band / DJ / Wedding Singer

Photographer

Videographer

Entertainment

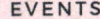

## NOTES

| MONDAY | TUESDAY | WEDNESDAY | THURSDAY | FRIDAY | SATURDAY | SUNDAY |
|--------|---------|-----------|----------|--------|----------|--------|
|        |         |           |          |        |          |        |
|        |         |           |          |        |          |        |
|        |         |           |          |        |          |        |
|        |         |           |          |        |          |        |
|        |         |           |          |        |          |        |

## EVENTS

## PRO TIP

If you've got a large venue, having a cordless microphone for any speeches can go a long way. Your speakers will feel more prepared and you'll avoid awkwardness as the mic moves around the room.

# VENDOR SELECTION
## MUSIC, PHOTO/VIDEOGRAPHER, ETC.

**Key Points**

Date

Arrival Time

Exit Time

Guest Count

Attire

Theme/Style

Priorities

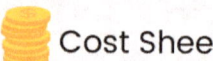 Cost Sheet

Music

Photographer

Videographer

Entertainment

Total

## Things to Consider

- Availability
- Reliability
- How their style matches yours
- See photographer's portfolio
- Watch a videographer's work
- Go see the band play live
- Any restrictions w/ the venue?
- Enough space at the venue?
- Band / DJ
  - Can play or learn your songs
  - Any needs from the venue?
  - Also available for Ceremony?
- Photographer & Videographer:
  - Key moments to capture
  - Key guests to capture
  - Overall tone of the footage

# NOTES

# 10 MONTHS
## Lay the Groundwork

### SHOP FOR THE DRESS

Give yourself plenty of time to try out different cuts and how they look on you. Do you prefer a Mermaid cut or an A-line? Trumpet or Sheath? Just keep in mind you should make the purchase at least 8 months before the day itself to ensure there's enough time for the dress to be made and alterations to be done.

### BLOCK HOTEL ROOMS FOR OUT-OF-TOWN GUESTS

You won't have an exact guest count yet but you can estimate about 70% of those invited will attend. Shoot for a hotel close to the reception venue so guests don't have a long trek after the big night. You will likely need to pay a sizable deposit to guarantee the rooms, but don't fret - you'll get that money back once your guests begin booking.

### GO DIGITAL

Simply the best way to compile all the essential information, prepare your guests and set the tone of your big day, wedding websites are ubiquitous these days. Several platforms allow you to easily craft a great looking site for a nominal price.

If your hotel block is not attached to your ceremony and reception venue, keep an eye out for hotels that provide shuttle service. You can always book a separate transportation provider, but you may be able to negotiate a better deal on this with the hotel.

# MONTH 10

### TO-DOS

Shop for the dress

Hotel room block

Website

_____

_____

### NOTES

| MONDAY | TUESDAY | WEDNESDAY | THURSDAY | FRIDAY | SATURDAY | SUNDAY |
|--------|---------|-----------|----------|--------|----------|--------|
|        |         |           |          |        |          |        |
|        |         |           |          |        |          |        |
|        |         |           |          |        |          |        |
|        |         |           |          |        |          |        |
|        |         |           |          |        |          |        |

### EVENTS

### PRO TIP

Wedding websites are a great tool to convey all your essential information. Just keep in mind that some guests will never click that link. Make sure your less tech-savvy guests are kept in the loop too!

# WEDDING WEBSITE
*Page Layout*

### HOME PAGE

A photo of the couple, your story, and the essential information like date, time, and location of the wedding.

### ITINERARY & RSVP

Time and location for all events. Most sites have a built in RSVP function to help you stay organized.

### ACCOMMODATION

The hotel room block along with booking instructions. If you are not blocking rooms, you can list any recommendations you have.

### TRAVEL

List the best airport to fly into, its 3-letter code, and give local restaurant, activity, or sight-seeing recommendations.

### WEDDING PARTY

List both sides of the wedding party and a quick blurb about who they are and their significance in your life.

### FAQ

Are children allowed at the ceremony? Plus-ones? Edit as often as you like to add any questions you are frequently being asked.

# WEDDING ATTIRE BUDGET

| DESCRIPTION | BUDGETED | ACTUAL COST | DEPOSIT |
|---|---|---|---|
| Dress | | | |
| Veil | | | |
| Garter | | | |
| Jewelry | | | |
| Other accessories | | | |
| Shoes | | | |
| | | | |
| Suit / Tux | | | |
| Cuff links & accessories | | | |
| Shoes | | | |
| Alterations | | | |
| | | | |
| | | | |
| | | | |
| | | | |
| | | | |
| | | | |
| | | | |
| | | | |
| | | | |
| | | | |
| **Total** | | | |

# 9 MONTHS
## The First Big Moves

### PURCHASE THE DRESS

Nine months is an ideal amount of time for your dress maker to work their magic while allowing plenty of time for alterations. If you're not quite ready for this decision, you've still got a month until crunch time.

### PLAN YOUR EVENTS

You've got your venue and caterer locked in, along with some of the essential vendors. Now it's time to get into the details of your ceremony and reception. Getting this taken care of now will give you a solid idea of how you're doing budget-wise and will help inform the decisions you'll be making over the next few months.

### SEND OUT SAVE THE DATES

While not essential, Save the Dates will get people excited and can result in early RSVPs. Sending now gives your guests time to get the best flight deals. If you're sending Save the Dates, it could help to consider all your stationery needs now. Think invitations, RSVP cards, thank you cards, place cards, the guest book and any signage. Ordering in bulk could reduce the price, and you'll ensure all your stationery has the same overall design style.

There are a lot of free graphic design programs online. If you're even the least bit crafty, you can design your own stationery and have it printed on high-quality paper, saving money without sacrificing quality.

# MONTH 9

## TO-DOS

- Purchase the dress
- Ceremony & Reception details
- Save the Date
- _____
- _____

## NOTES

| MONDAY | TUESDAY | WEDNESDAY | THURSDAY | FRIDAY | SATURDAY | SUNDAY |
|--------|---------|-----------|----------|--------|----------|--------|
|        |         |           |          |        |          |        |
|        |         |           |          |        |          |        |
|        |         |           |          |        |          |        |
|        |         |           |          |        |          |        |
|        |         |           |          |        |          |        |

## EVENTS

## PRO TIP

Confirm your venue's maximum capacity, check in with your budget, and give your guest list a critical look before sending Save the Dates. A bloated guest list hurts; you can always invite additional guests later.

# Ceremony
## Key Elements

### PLANNING YOUR OWN CEREMONY?

Below are the typical elements found in an American wedding ceremony in their usual order of appearance. If you're going the traditional route, your officiant will likely take care of this. If you're planning your own ceremony or blending elements of multiple wedding traditions, you can use this as a rough guide for the flow. The only real requirement is that your ceremony feels right to you. Your guests will appreciate any heartfelt personal touches. It's your time to shine!

- [ ] Entrance music - as guests are seated
- [ ] Entrance music - as wedding party walks down the aisle
- [ ] Entrance song - as you walk down the aisle
- [ ] Welcome
- [ ] Introduction of the couple
- [ ] Readings
- [ ] Confirmation you both will uphold the marriage
- [ ] Reading of the vows
- [ ] Exchanging rings
- [ ] Kiss
- [ ] Closing words
- [ ] Recessional -as you and the wedding party exits

# CEREMONY
## PLANNING SHEET

**Venue & Contact:**

---

**Time:**

**Date:**

**Guest Count:**

**Officiant:**

**Music:**

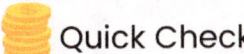 **Quick Check**

Venue

Officiant

Music

Decoration

Rentals

Extras

**Total**

**To Do:**

- Choose the style and flow
- Finalize the guest list
- Select the venue
- Hire your officiant
- Obtain your marriage license
- Prelude music: as guests sit
- Entrance music: wedding party
- Entrance music: the couple
- Sound system / microphones
- Furniture rentals
- Flowers
- Decorations
- Arrange transportation

# CEREMONY BUDGET

| DESCRIPTION | BUDGETED | ACTUAL COST | DEPOSIT |
|---|---|---|---|
| Venue Rental | | | |
| Officiant | | | |
| Venue Coordinator | | | |
| Decoration | | | |
| Flowers | | | |
|     To be held and worn | | | |
|     Petals to be thrown | | | |
|     Venue decoration | | | |
|     Extra | | | |
| Rentals | | | |
|     Chairs | | | |
|     Lighting | | | |
|     Sound Equipment | | | |
|     Extras | | | |
| Music | | | |
| Transportation | | | |
| | | | |
| | | | |
| | | | |
| | | | |
| | | | |
| | | | |
| **Total** | | | |

# RECEPTION
## PLANNING SHEET

**Venue & Contact:**

**Start & End:**

**Date:**

**Guest Count:**

**Attire:**

**Theme:**

**Music:**

**Menu:**

**Drinks:**

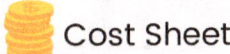 **Cost Sheet**

Food & Beverage

Staff

Music & Sound

Decoration

Rentals

Extras

**Total**

**To Do:**

- [ ] Choose the style and theme
- [ ] Finalize the guest list
- [ ] Confirm the venue
- [ ] Cocktail Hour / Hors D'oeuvres
- [ ] Finalize the dinner menu
- [ ] Select bar service
- [ ] Hire the musicians
- [ ] Sound system & microphones
- [ ] Furniture rentals
- [ ] Floral decorations
- [ ] Other decorations
- [ ] Photographer & Videographer
- [ ] Gifts for the wedding party
- [ ] Party Favors
- [ ] Guest parking / Valet
- [ ] Transportation to & from
- [ ]
- [ ]
- [ ]

# RECEPTION BUDGET

| DESCRIPTION | BUDGETED | ACTUAL COST | DEPOSIT |
|---|---|---|---|
| Venue Rental | | | |
| Planner / Coordinator | | | |
| Catering | | | |
|    Reception hors d'oeuvres | | | |
|    Dinner | | | |
|    Beverages | | | |
|    Staff | | | |
|    Tax & Gratuities | | | |
| Flowers | | | |
|    Venue Decoration | | | |
|    Bouquets | | | |
|    Centerpieces | | | |
|    Delivery/Extras | | | |
| Non-floral Decorations | | | |
| Photographer / Videographer | | | |
| Rentals | | | |
|    Tables & Chairs | | | |
|    Cocktail / Lounge Furniture | | | |
|    Linens / Tableware | | | |
|    Lighting / Sound Equipment | | | |
|    Sound Equipment | | | |
|    Dance Floor | | | |
|    Extras | | | |

# RECEPTION BUDGET CONT.

| DESCRIPTION | BUDGETED | ACTUAL COST | DEPOSIT |
|---|---|---|---|
| **Hair & Makeup** | | | |
| Couple | | | |
| Wedding Party & Family | | | |
| **Wedding Cake** | | | |
| Cake | | | |
| Cutting Fee | | | |
| Rentals (knives, cake stand, etc.) | | | |
| Delivery | | | |
| **Wedding Attire** | | | |
| Dresses | | | |
| Suits | | | |
| Shoes | | | |
| Extras | | | |
| **Transportation** | | | |
| Shuttles | | | |
| Couple & Wedding Party | | | |
| Getaway Car | | | |
| **Gifts for the Wedding Party** | | | |
| **Party Favors** | | | |
| **Tips / Gratuities** | | | |
| | | | |
| | | | |
| **Total** | | | |

# 8 MONTHS
## Florals and Wedding Party

### SELECTING A FLORIST

Deciding on your florist goes beyond their jaw-dropping arrangements. It is crucial they can deliver a flawless execution. Are they experienced with large events and do they have sufficient staff to decorate the venue on schedule? You'll benefit from an experienced florist who has suggestions for staying on budget while designing for maximum effect.

### THE WEDDING PARTY

Eight months out is a good time to discuss who you would like to be standing at your side as you tie the knot. Depending on the venue, 3-5 people on each side avoids crowding, but there are no rules here - you do you! On that note, we're increasingly seeing Groomsmaids, Mates of Honor, and the like showing up in wedding parties. Feel free to open up the playing field if that makes it easier to include those closest to you!

### WEDDING PARTY ATTIRE

You've selected the style and theme of the wedding, the color scheme is being refined as you speak with florists, and the wedding dress is on its way. These tasks complete, you've got the guidance you need to select what your wedding party will wear. It's a good idea to get the ball rolling for any dresses now. Suits take less time to source, so that will come later.

# MONTH 8

## TO-DOS

Florist

Wedding Party

Wedding Party dresses

_____

_____

## NOTES

| MONDAY | TUESDAY | WEDNESDAY | THURSDAY | FRIDAY | SATURDAY | SUNDAY |
|--------|---------|-----------|----------|--------|----------|--------|
|        |         |           |          |        |          |        |
|        |         |           |          |        |          |        |
|        |         |           |          |        |          |        |
|        |         |           |          |        |          |        |
|        |         |           |          |        |          |        |

## EVENTS

## PRO TIP

It is shockingly common that members of a wedding party are surprised to learn they are included! Make sure to approach everyone in your wedding party individually and confirm they're able to commit.

# FLORIST MEETING

**Florist:**                    **Contact:**

---

❖

---

- What experience to you have designing in our style?
- Do you have sufficient staff to cover all your events that day?
- Any photos of previous work you have done in this style?
- Any suggestions you have for achieving my vision on budget?
- What can you recommend that is in season that fits in with my style?
- Have you done a wedding at our venue before?
- Can you achieve our vision at this venue?
- Any other decorative items you provide (vases, votives, lighting, etc.)?
- Will you coordinate directly with the venue for installation?
- Is the delivery fee, set up and break down included in your rate?
- By when do we need to finalize the details?
- How much is the deposit and when is it due?
- Could you make an itemized list of all we've discussed and the cost?
- When is the final payment due?

## COST SHEET

| | |
|---|---|
| Centerpieces | $ |
| Bouquets & items to be worn | $ |
| Venue decoration | $ |
| Other decorative items | $ |
| Ceremony structure | $ |
| Delivery, set up and breakdown | $ |
| **Total** | $ |

# NOTES

# WEDDING PARTY

## CONSIDERATIONS FOR CHOOSING YOUR WEDDING PARTY

- Responsible & available
- Easy-going
- Supportive
- Collaborative Group Dynamic
- Gives their honest opinion
- Can give a good toast
- Self-sufficient
- Helpful
- Has a good relationship with both of you

_____'S PARTY      _____'S PARTY

| | |
|---|---|
| | |
| | |
| | |
| | |
| | |
| | |

# 7 MONTHS
## Welcoming Your Guests

### REHEARSAL DINNER

A rehearsal dinner traditionally follows the actual ceremony rehearsal, one day prior to the wedding. Invites are limited to the family of both sides, the wedding party, your officiant, and any out of town guests.

### WELCOME PARTY

If you'd like to break the ice between both sides before the big night, some couples opt for a welcome party instead of, or in addition to the Rehearsal Dinner. It's the same basic concept, but with a more open invitation and less formal. Think a cocktail party with passed appetizers, a backyard BBQ, or booking the back room of a bar or casual restaurant.

### HANDLING THE RENTALS

If you've chosen a venue that is accustomed to weddings, this will be easy. Let's say you've gone for something unique like a barn or villa for the ceremony and reception; you'll need chairs, tables and decorations. Perhaps plates, silverware and glasses. Cocktail tables and lounge furniture are great to consider for guests who won't be shaking it on the dance floor all night. Does your decorating style beg for torches, string lights, or the like? Oh, and don't forget a dance floor!

### BUDGET TIPS

Some items are cheaper to buy than to rent. Look out for deals on lighting, tableware, decorations, even sound equipment. Wedding vendors apply a drastic upcharge to these items.

If your ceremony and reception will take place at the same venue, see if there's a logical way to use the same chairs for both. Staff can set them at tables once the ceremony is over.

# MONTH 7

## TO-DOS

Welcome party

Rehearsal dinner

Rental items

_____

_____

## NOTES

| MONDAY | TUESDAY | WEDNESDAY | THURSDAY | FRIDAY | SATURDAY | SUNDAY |
|--------|---------|-----------|----------|--------|----------|--------|
|        |         |           |          |        |          |        |
|        |         |           |          |        |          |        |
|        |         |           |          |        |          |        |
|        |         |           |          |        |          |        |
|        |         |           |          |        |          |        |

## EVENTS

## PRO TIP

You're probably feeling the budget pain now. As the price starts ballooning, try to stay grounded. Next month it's time for the budget check-in, and you can adjust then. For now, stay realistic but dream big while you're planning.

# REHEARSAL DINNER
## PLANNING SHEET

**Venue & Contact:**

**Start & End:**

**Date:**

**Guest Count:**

**Attire:**

**Theme:**

**Music:**

**Menu:**

**Drinks:**

 ## Cost Sheet

Food & Beverage

Staff

Music & Sound

Decoration

Rentals

Extras

**Total**

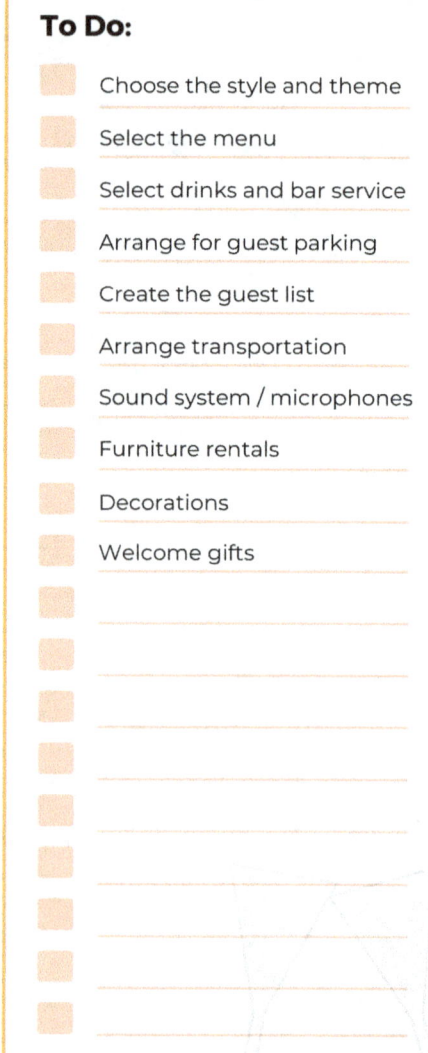

**To Do:**

- Choose the style and theme
- Select the menu
- Select drinks and bar service
- Arrange for guest parking
- Create the guest list
- Arrange transportation
- Sound system / microphones
- Furniture rentals
- Decorations
- Welcome gifts

# REHEARSAL DINNER BUDGET

| DESCRIPTION | BUDGETED | ACTUAL COST | DEPOSIT |
|---|---|---|---|
| Venue Rental | | | |
| Planner / Coordinator | | | |
| Catering | | | |
| Hors d'oeuvres | | | |
| Dinner | | | |
| Beverages | | | |
| Staff | | | |
| Tax & Gratuities | | | |
| Decoration | | | |
| Rentals | | | |
| Tables & Chairs | | | |
| Cocktail / Lounge Furniture | | | |
| Linens / Tableware | | | |
| Lighting | | | |
| Sound Equipment | | | |
| Dance Floor | | | |
| Extras | | | |
| Music | | | |
| Entertainment | | | |
| Transportation | | | |
| | | | |
| | | | |
| **Total** | | | |

# WELCOME PARTY
## PLANNING SHEET

**Venue & Contact:**

**Start & End:**

**Date:**

**Guest Count:**

**Attire:**

**Theme:**

**Music:**

**Menu:**

**Drinks:**

 **Cost Sheet**

Food & Beverage

Staff

Music & Sound

Decoration

Rentals

Extras

**Total**

**To Do:**

- Choose the style and theme
- Select the menu
- Select drinks and bar service
- Arrange for guest parking
- Create the guest list
- Arrange transportation
- Sound system / microphones
- Furniture rentals
- Decorations
- Welcome gifts

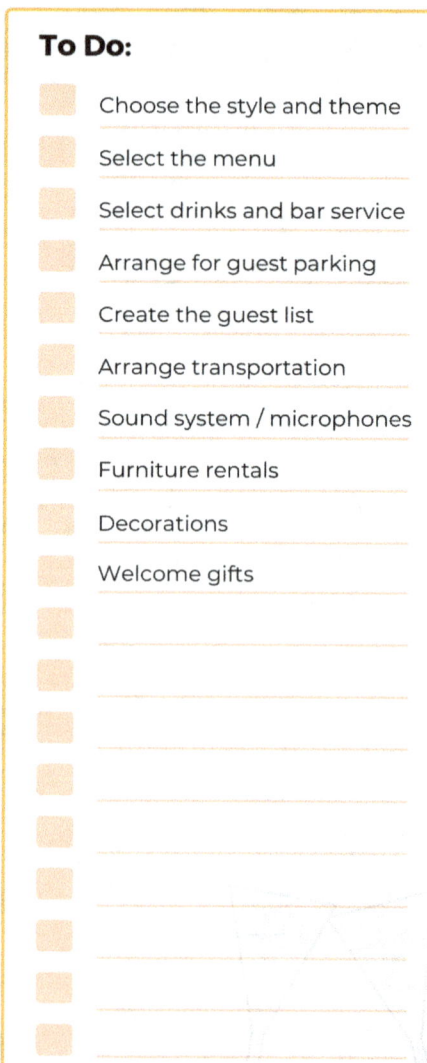

# WELCOME PARTY BUDGET

| DESCRIPTION | BUDGETED | ACTUAL COST | DEPOSIT |
|---|---|---|---|
| Venue Rental | | | |
| Planner / Coordinator | | | |
| Catering | | | |
| Hors d'oeuvres | | | |
| Dinner | | | |
| Beverages | | | |
| Staff | | | |
| Tax & Gratuities | | | |
| Decoration | | | |
| Rentals | | | |
| Tables & Chairs | | | |
| Cocktail tables | | | |
| Lounge Furniture | | | |
| Lighting | | | |
| Sound Equipment | | | |
| Linens / Tableware | | | |
| Extras | | | |
| Music | | | |
| Entertainment | | | |
| Transportation | | | |
| | | | |
| | | | |
| **Total** | | | |

# 6 MONTHS
## A Little Breather

### BUDGET CHECK-IN

By now you've got a pretty accurate picture of what your wedding is going to cost you. There are a few more expenses over the coming months, but the heavy hitters are taken care of. How is your budget stacking up? The most impactful way to trim cost is likely your catering budget per head.

### GET IN THE HONEYMOON MOOD

You've spent the past few months thinking of how you'll manage your guests, so now think about the two of you for a minute! Think about some dream locations for your honeymoon, do a little research, and start plotting your first big *married* adventure.

### GIFT REGISTRY

You don't need to have this completely locked in already, but now is the time  to at least get the ball rolling. It's a good idea to add your gift registry information to a new page on your wedding website to make things easy for everyone.

### STAY SANE!

Don't be shy in asking trusted friends and family to step in and help where they can. In the event there is someone stepping on your toes or interjecting where you'd rather they didn't, there's no better time than now to have a heartfelt conversation. There will be tasks in the coming months (venue walk-through, final tasting, day-of coordination) where they will come in handy if you choose to include them.

# MONTH 6

## TO-DOS

Budget check in

Honeymoon plan

Gift registry

_____

_____

## NOTES

| MONDAY | TUESDAY | WEDNESDAY | THURSDAY | FRIDAY | SATURDAY | SUNDAY |
|--------|---------|-----------|----------|--------|----------|--------|
|        |         |           |          |        |          |        |
|        |         |           |          |        |          |        |
|        |         |           |          |        |          |        |
|        |         |           |          |        |          |        |
|        |         |           |          |        |          |        |

## EVENTS

## PRO TIP

People sometimes forget boundaries when someone they love is planning their wedding. Your friends or relatives may become controlling. Get ahead of it by setting limits on their influence early and gently.

# 5 MONTHS
## The Suits & Transportation

### GUEST SHUTTLES

See if the hotels you've chosen provide a shuttle service - or if you can negotiate this. While you're at it, think about any out of town guests that might need special assistance arranging their transportation.

### LIMOUSINES AND THE GETAWAY

You'll need reliable transportation the day of the wedding, and be sure not to omit your wedding party when mulling over the logistics. Increasingly trendy is the couple riding in the same vehicle as the full wedding party, be it limo, party bus, or something even more creative. This keeps everyone on the same schedule and allows for a bit of celebration before the wedding. While you're at it, you may as well consider the getaway car or how you'll make your grand exit!

### GET SUITED AND BOOTED

Suit or Tux? Rent or buy? Maybe use something that's already in the closet? Five months out is a good time to make the necessary arrangements for the suit. This gives you plenty time to try different styles and get alterations done before the big day.

# MONTH 5

## TO-DOS

Guest transportation

Transportation for the couple

Purchase suits

_____

_____

## NOTES

| MONDAY | TUESDAY | WEDNESDAY | THURSDAY | FRIDAY | SATURDAY | SUNDAY |
|--------|---------|-----------|----------|--------|----------|--------|
|        |         |           |          |        |          |        |
|        |         |           |          |        |          |        |
|        |         |           |          |        |          |        |
|        |         |           |          |        |          |        |
|        |         |           |          |        |          |        |

## EVENTS

## PRO TIP

Be sure to negotiate rates with transportation providers, especially if you're booking several vehicles. Get clear on any extra charges that will come on top of your price quote - gas, mileage, gratuity, anything at all.

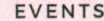

# TRANSPORTATION
*Logistics*

## THE COUPLE

Vehicle type:

Pickup time:

Pickup address:

Location 1:

Location 2:

Location 3:

Details:

## WEDDING PARTY

Vehicle type:

No. Passengers:

Pickup time:

Pickup address:

Location 1:

Location 2:

Location 3:

Details:

## HOTEL:

No. Passengers:

Pickup time:

Drop off:

Details:

## HOTEL:

No. Passengers:

Pickup time:

Drop off:

Details:

## HOTEL:

No. Passengers:

Pickup time:

Drop off:

Details:

# TRANSPORTATION BUDGET

| DESCRIPTION | BUDGETED | ACTUAL COST | DEPOSIT |
|---|---|---|---|
| Transportation: couple | | | |
| Transportation: wedding party | | | |
| Transportation: additional | | | |
| Getaway car | | | |
| Hotel Shuttles | | | |
| Valet | | | |
| | | | |
| | | | |
| | | | |
| | | | |
| | | | |
| | | | |
| | | | |
| | | | |
| | | | |
| | | | |
| | | | |
| | | | |
| | | | |
| Fuel | | | |
| Mileage | | | |
| Tips / Gratuities | | | |
| **Total** | | | |

# 4 MONTHS
## Tasty Tasks

### FINAL TASTING WITH THE CATERER

Who doesn't love a good menu tasting? This isn't always as fun as it sounds, though. Emotions can run high as you chew on the fact that all of the most important people in your life will be enjoying this meal together. You may want to bring a neutral 3rd party along to chime in. This is a *great* way to involve anyone that's pushing to exert influence, as long as they're objective and will defer to you for the final decision.

### CHOOSE YOUR WEDDING CAKE

Selecting a baker is like any other vendor - they'll need to have great style along with the professionalism to pull off the execution. Things like delivery, display, and any special care instructions will be crucial to understand. The questions in this section will help you align on your priorities with potential bakers.

### GET THE WEDDING BANDS COVERED

Maybe you've already handled this. If not, now's the time to go jewelry shopping. Plenty of alternatives to silver and gold are out there, and it's a good idea to choose rings that are easy to maintain and well suited to withstand the wear and tear demanded by each person's lifestyle.

# MONTH 4

## TO-DOS

Final tasting

Wedding cake

Wedding rings

_____

_____

## NOTES

| MONDAY | TUESDAY | WEDNESDAY | THURSDAY | FRIDAY | SATURDAY | SUNDAY |
|--------|---------|-----------|----------|--------|----------|--------|
|        |         |           |          |        |          |        |
|        |         |           |          |        |          |        |
|        |         |           |          |        |          |        |
|        |         |           |          |        |          |        |
|        |         |           |          |        |          |        |

## EVENTS

## PRO TIP

With a plethora of options beyond just silver and gold, couples are increasingly choosing wedding bands made of unique materials. Make sure whatever you choose is practical and able to be re-sized as time goes on.

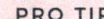

# BAKER MEETING

**Bakery:**                    **Contact:**

---

- How many weddings do you do in a typical year?
- Have you done this type of cake design before?
- How will the cake be displayed?
- Do you have cake stands, toppers or other decorative items for rent?
- What are the additional fees for the rentals?
- How soon before the wedding will you bake the cake?
- When and how will the delivery arrive?
- Are there any special care instructions upon arrival?
- By when do we need to place the final order?
- What is the delivery fee?
- When is the deposit and final payment due?

## COST SHEET

| | |
|---|---|
| Cake | $ |
| Toppers | $ |
| Cake Stand | $ |
| Knives | $ |
| Other Rentals | $ |
| Delivery | $ |
| **Total** | $ |

# NOTES

# 3 MONTHS
## Begin Finalizing

### SEND THE INVITATIONS

Etiquette is for guests to receive invitations anywhere from 6 weeks to 5 months before the event. Invitations should include an RSVP response card and return envelope, along with Rehearsal Dinner invitations for anyone included in that event.

### FINALIZE THE MENU

Make your final choices for what will be served and the exact timing. This is especially important if you've got multiple moving parts such as a cocktail hour before the reception or any furniture movements throughout the night. It pays to ask your caterer to create an itemized list and the schedule to make sure you're aligned.

### SPEAKING FROM THE HEART

Who will be giving a speech or toast? You'll want to give them them plenty of time to start word crafting, so asking them 3 months prior is a good move. You two should also start writing your vows at this point. Give yourself time to practice out loud before the big day!

### CHOOSING YOUR OFFICIANT

Whether you're going the traditional route or planning something more personalized, the officiant should have some basic qualifications: they can lawfully marry you, they can speak a few words about you as a couple, and their presence fits in with your overall style and theme.

# MONTH 3

## TO-DOS

Send invitations

Finalize the menu

Ask for speeches / toasts

Begin writing your vows

Select your officiant

## NOTES

| MONDAY | TUESDAY | WEDNESDAY | THURSDAY | FRIDAY | SATURDAY | SUNDAY |
|--------|---------|-----------|----------|--------|----------|--------|
|        |         |           |          |        |          |        |
|        |         |           |          |        |          |        |
|        |         |           |          |        |          |        |
|        |         |           |          |        |          |        |
|        |         |           |          |        |          |        |

## EVENTS

## PRO TIP

When designing your invitations, you could include a QR code that links directly to the RSVP page of your wedding website. It's a handy way to remind guests of all the information available to them and makes it easy to RSVP.

# 2 MONTHS
## Dress Fitting, Party Essentials

### DRESS FITTING

Your dress should be ready for its first fitting now. Your final fitting should be scheduled during the two weeks prior to the wedding. While you're at it, you can purchase the veil, garter or any extra accessories.

### MARRIAGE LICENSE

A simple bureaucratic moment not to be overlooked. Learn any specific details about how soon before the wedding you should take care of this, as it varies from state to state.

### PARTY FAVORS & WEDDING PARTY GIFTS

Will you send your guests home with a small keepsake? This shouldn't be a large budget item, but it is nice to send people off with a little memento. If you're having a destination wedding or the majority of your guests are from out of town, a welcome bag at the hotel is a great touch. As for your wedding party, things like engraved flasks, robes, and jewelry are common. These gifts are best when they're personalized, heart-felt and functional.

### FLORAL MOCKUP

The level of detail you'll get here will depend on your florist, but take a moment to get a very clear vision of their plan and make any tweaks. Confirm the delivery time, how setup will be handled, and any special care instructions.

# MONTH 2

## TO-DOS

Dress fitting

Marriage license

Party favors

Floral mockup

_____

## NOTES

| MONDAY | TUESDAY | WEDNESDAY | THURSDAY | FRIDAY | SATURDAY | SUNDAY |
|--------|---------|-----------|----------|--------|----------|--------|
|        |         |           |          |        |          |        |
|        |         |           |          |        |          |        |
|        |         |           |          |        |          |        |
|        |         |           |          |        |          |        |
|        |         |           |          |        |          |        |

## EVENTS

## PRO TIP

On the party favors, think about your wedding's theme, location, or any other unique qualities. Are there practical items or local specialties that you like? Beautiful hand fans, local sweets, or ceramics are a start!

# FINAL MONTH
## Organize and Delegate

### FINALIZE THE PLAN

Create the run of show for the entire day of the wedding. Use the template in this section to get things in order, and keep in mind things always take longer than you would expect. Build in some buffer time. You'll want to print several copies of this schedule for your photographer, venue manager and anyone helping to organize logistics the day of the wedding. Walk through your venue and play out that schedule, keeping a critical eye out for any potential friction points.

### SEATING CHART

Any RSVPs that have not been received by now need to be chased, both for the caterer's final head count and for your seating chart. Sit down as a couple and draft up the seating chart, leaving room for some stragglers to continue to RSVP.

### SEND YOUR SONG LIST TO THE BAND / DJ

Think about the entrance music for the ceremony, the song you'll walk down the aisle to, your first dance, the parent dance, and the final song that closes out the night. Confirming this song list early is especially important with a live band to ensure they've got time to practice.

### ENLIST SOME HELP

It is crucial to select a point person for the day-of. They should be your right hand by knowing the schedule and being self-sufficient enough to coordinate with vendors and handle all the deliveries and setup. Avoid being the point person for anything - you'll be busy enough.

# MONTH 1

### TO-DOS

- Run of show
- Final venue walk-through
- Seating chart
- Song list to DJ / Band
- Break your shoes in!

### NOTES

| MONDAY | TUESDAY | WEDNESDAY | THURSDAY | FRIDAY | SATURDAY | SUNDAY |
|--------|---------|-----------|----------|--------|----------|--------|
| 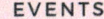 | | | | | | |
| | | | | | | |
| | | | | | | |
| | | | | | | |
| | | | | | | |

### EVENTS

### PRO TIP

When enlisting help for the day-of, don't overlook the end of the night. There will be a lot to manage: decorations, flowers, gifts, and more. You'll be exhausted so it's good to have some help lined up.

# SAMPLE DAY-OF RUN OF SHOW

| EVENT | TIME | POINT PERSON |
|---|---|---|
| Pre-ceremony photos | | |
| *Buffer* | | |
| Ceremony start time on invitations | | |
| True ceremony start time | | |
| *Buffer* | | |
| Cocktail hour | | |
| Welcome toasts | | |
| *Buffer* | | |
| Dinner | | |
| First dance | | |
| Speeches and toasts | | |
| *Buffer* | | |
| Parent dance | | |
| Cake cutting | | |
| Your big exit | | |
| | | |
| | | |
| | | |
| | | |
| | | |
| | | |
| | | |
| | | |

# SAMPLE VENDOR MASTER SHEET

| VENDOR & POINT PERSON | ARRIVAL TIME | PHONE # |
|---|---|---|
| Planner | | |
| Photographer | | |
| Venue coordinator | | |
| Florist | | |
| Caterer | | |
| Rental furniture | | |
| Musician | | |
| Wedding cake | | |
| Officiant | | |
| | | |
| | | |
| | | |

| ADDITIONAL GRATUITIES | POINT PERSON | ENVELOPE RECIEVED |
|---|---|---|
| Officiant | | |
| Photographer's crew | | |
| Videographer's crew | | |
| Wait staff | | |
| Bar staff | | |
| Caterer / Banquet Manager | | |
| Hair | | |
| Makeup | | |
| Band | | |
| Transportation | | |

# Example Seating Chart

TABLE #    TABLE #    TABLE #

TABLE #    TABLE #    TABLE #

TABLE #    TABLE #    TABLE #

TABLE #    TABLE #    TABLE #

TABLE #    TABLE #    TABLE #

TABLE #    TABLE #    TABLE #

# 1 WEEK OUT
## Prepare and Pamper

### PAMPER YOURSELF

It pays to have some beauty appointments booked. You deserve a little self care by now, and you'll want to go into your wedding day looking fresh and feeling great. Take a chance to connect with each other in a non-pressurized environment. A quiet dinner date or a couples massage can do wonders!

### MAKE FINAL VENDOR PAYMENTS

You should make your final payments this week. While you're at it, you can confirm their arrival time to avoid any miscommunication. Put any tips in individual envelopes and label the recipient. This makes it easy for you or your point person to distribute them on the day-of.

### PACK YOUR HONEYMOON BAGS

Get into the zone! Pack your bags and enjoy a little daydream about the paradise you'll be spending your honeymoon in.

### TICK OFF THE CHECKLISTS

There are checklists on the next few pages for this week, the night before, and the day of your wedding. Tick off all the boxes, relish in the fact that you've just organized the event of a lifetime, and go into your wedding day feeling great!

# FINAL WEEK

## WEEKLY PRIORITIES

- Pay vendors in full
- Put tips in individual envelopes
- Finalize vendor schedule
- Pamper yourself
- _____

### Notes

| Monday | Tuesday | Wednesday | Thursday | Friday | Saturday | Sunday |
|--------|---------|-----------|----------|--------|----------|--------|
|        |         |           |          |        |          |        |

## Checklist

- ☐ _____
- ☐ _____
- ☐ _____
- ☐ _____
- ☐ _____
- ☐ _____
- ☐ _____
- ☐ _____
- ☐ _____
- ☐ _____
- ☐ _____

## Appointment

## Reminder

# Week of the Wedding
## Checklist

- [ ] Refresh your hair cut and color. No big changes!
- [ ] Get eyebrows done
- [ ] Get a facial
- [ ] Have a mani-pedi
- [ ] Final dress fitting (bring a bridesmaid)
- [ ] Pack your honeymoon bags
- [ ] Practice your vows out loud
- [ ] Bachelor and bachelorette party
- [ ] Take time off from work
- [ ] Couples massage
- [ ] Have a quiet date night together
- [ ] Chase any lagging RSVPs with a vengeance

# The Night Before
# Checklist

❖

- Pack the car for tomorrow
  - Wedding rings
  - Printed vows & marriage license
  - Extra shoes and outfit
  - Tips for vendors in individual, labeled envelopes
  - Multiple copies of your wedding day run of show
  - The honeymoon bag
- Pack a personal bag
  - Extra makeup, hair ties, hygiene products
  - Band-aids, pain relievers, deodorant
  - Safety pins, lint roller, needle & thread
  - Snacks
- Have a healthy dinner and plenty of water
- Shut off your phone and go to bed early

# The Day-of
# Checklist

Your paragraph text

- Wake up early
- Have a healthy breakfast
- Drink plenty of water all day
- Lay out your outfits - do they need steaming?
- Write each other a cute little note
- Say "thank you" often
- Touch base with your point person
- Breathe deep and enjoy today to its fullest!

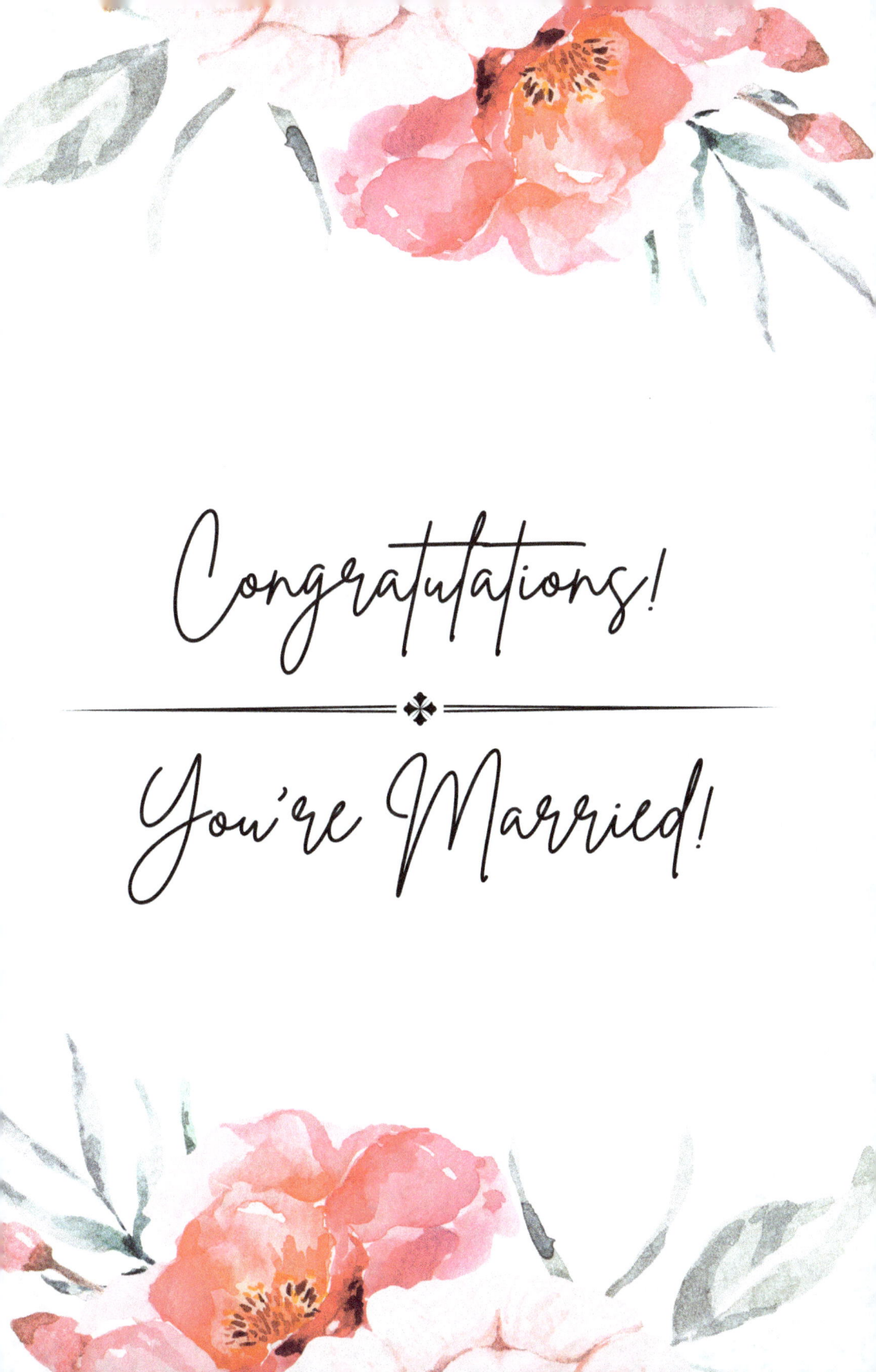

*Congratulations!*

❖

*You're Married!*